4th Grade Workbooks

Measurement & Division Practice

Speedy Publishing LLC
40 E. Main St. #1156
Newark, DE 19711
www.speedypublishing.com

DIVISION

$14\overline{)420}$

$14\overline{)238}$

$13\overline{)377}$

$10\overline{)300}$

$5\overline{)130}$

$15\overline{)270}$

DIVISION

11 ⟌ 297	9 ⟌ 144	10 ⟌ 230
11 ⟌ 176	14 ⟌ 252	8 ⟌ 208

DIVISION

$6 \overline{)126}$ $14 \overline{)406}$ $15 \overline{)270}$

$11 \overline{)242}$ $12 \overline{)192}$ $9 \overline{)252}$

DIVISION

7 ⟌ 147	8 ⟌ 216	8 ⟌ 192
14 ⟌ 294	9 ⟌ 216	8 ⟌ 160

DIVISION

$15 \overline{)450}$	$5 \overline{)100}$	$8 \overline{)128}$
$7 \overline{)210}$	$11 \overline{)264}$	$10 \overline{)250}$

DIVISION

8 ⟌ 152	9 ⟌ 162	13 ⟌ 338
8 ⟌ 208	12 ⟌ 360	13 ⟌ 299

DIVISION

8 ⟌ 160

8 ⟌ 168

13 ⟌ 273

7 ⟌ 168

14 ⟌ 322

8 ⟌ 120

DIVISION

10 ⟌ 190	10 ⟌ 260	6 ⟌ 156
14 ⟌ 266	8 ⟌ 128	13 ⟌ 273

DIVISION

$8\overline{)120}$ $12\overline{)216}$ $15\overline{)405}$

$6\overline{)90}$ $9\overline{)243}$ $12\overline{)288}$

DIVISION

$8 \overline{)176}$ $14 \overline{)392}$ $12 \overline{)288}$

$12 \overline{)252}$ $15 \overline{)405}$ $7 \overline{)175}$

DIVISION

$11\overline{)330}$ $14\overline{)378}$ $13\overline{)260}$

$5\overline{)75}$ $9\overline{)252}$ $7\overline{)161}$

DIVISION

15) 270

10) 250

14) 266

15) 450

7) 189

7) 161

MEASUREMENT

Research and fill in the correct answer.
Show your solutions.

1. 24 inches = ________ foot

2. 4 feet = ________ inches

MEASUREMENT

Research and fill in the correct answer.
Show your solutions.

3. 6 inches = _______ foot

4. 148 centimeters = _______ meters

MEASUREMENT

Research and fill in the correct answer.
Show your solutions.

5. 22 meters = ________ centimeters

6. 22.44 kilometers = ________ meter

MEASUREMENT

Research and fill in the correct answer.
Show your solutions.

7. 67.3 kilometers = ________ meter

8. 60320 meters = ________ kilometers

MEASUREMENT

Research and fill in the correct answer.
Show your solutions.

9. 54700 meters = ________ kilometers

10. 47 kilometers = ________ meter

MEASUREMENT

Research and fill in the correct answer.
Show your solutions.

11. 868 meters = ________ yards

12. 96800 meters = ________ kilometers

MEASUREMENT

Research and fill in the correct answer.
Show your solutions.

13. 18430 meters = ________ kilometers

14. 968 meters = ________ kilometers

MEASUREMENT

Research and fill in the correct answer. Show your solutions.

15. 184 millimeters = ________ yards

16. 899 meters = ________ millimeters

MEASUREMENT

Research and fill in the correct answer.
Show your solutions.

17. 168 feet = ________ meters

18. 483 feet = ________ meters

MEASUREMENT

Research and fill in the correct answer.
Show your solutions.

19. 448 meters = ________ feet

20. 646 meters = ________ yards

MEASUREMENT

Research and fill in the correct answer.
Show your solutions.

21. 316 kilometers = ________ meters

22. 113 yards = ________ centimeters

MEASUREMENT

Research and fill in the correct answer.
Show your solutions.

23. 204 centimeters = ________ feet

24. 113 yards = ________ centimeters

ANSWERS

420 / 14 = **30**
300 / 10 = **30**
297 / 11 = **27**
176 / 11 = **16**
126 / 6 = **21**
242 / 11 = **22**
147 / 7 = **21**
294 / 14 = **21**
450 / 15 = **30**
210 / 7 = **30**
152 / 8 = **19**
208 / 8 = **26**

238 / 14 = **17**
130 / 5 = **26**
144 / 9 = **16**
252 / 14 = **18**
406 / 14 = **29**
192 / 12 = **16**
216 / 8 = **27**
216 / 9 = **24**
100 / 5 = **20**
264 / 11 = **24**
162 / 9 = **18**
360 / 12 = **30**

377 / 13 = **29**
270 / 15 = **18**
230 / 10 = **23**
208 / 8 = **26**
270 / 15 = **18**
252 / 9 = **28**
192 / 8 = **24**
160 / 8 = **20**
128 / 8 = **16**
250 / 10 = **25**
338 / 13 = **26**
299 / 13 = **23**

160 / 8 = **20**

168 / 7 = **24**

190 / 10 = **19**

266 / 14 = **19**

120 / 8 = **15**

90 / 6 = **15**

176 / 8 = **22**

252 / 12 = **21**

330 / 11 = **30**

75 / 5 = **15**

270 / 15 = **18**

450 / 15 **30**

168 / 8 = **21**

322 / 14 = **23**

260 / 10 = **26**

128 / 8 = **16**

216 / 12 = **18**

243 / 9 = **27**

392 / 14 = **28**

405 / 15 = **27**

378 / 14 = **27**

252 / 9 = **28**

250 / 10 = **25**

189 / 7 **27**

273 / 13 = **21**

120 / 8 = **15**

156 / 6 = **26**

273 / 13 = **21**

405 / 15 = **27**

288 / 12 = **24**

288 / 12 = **24**

175 / 7 = **25**

260 / 13 = **20**

161 / 7 = **23**

266 / 14 = **19**

161 / 7 **23**

1. 24 inches = 2 ft

2. 4 feet = 48 inches

3. 6 inches = 1/2 ft

4. 148 centimeters = 1.48 meters

5. 22 meters = 2200 centimeters

6. 22.44 kilometers = 22440 meter

7. 67.3 kilometers = 67300 meter

8. 60320 meters = 60.32 kilometers

9. 54700 meters = 54.7 kilometers

10. 47 kilometers = 47000 meter

11. 868 meters = 949.25 yards

12. 96800 meters = 96.8 kilometers

13. 18430 meters = 18.430 kilometers

14. 968 meters = .968 kilometers

15. 184 millimeters = 0.20 yards

16. 899 meters = 899000 millimeters

17. 168 feet = 51.21 meters

18. 483 feet = 147.22 meters

19. 448 meters = 1469.82 feet

20. 646 meters = 706.47 yards

21. 316 kilometers = 316000 meters

22. 113 yards = 10332.72 centimeters

23. 204 centimeters = 6.69 feet

24. 110 yards = 10058.4 centimeters

www.ingramcontent.com/pod-product-compliance
Lightning Source LLC
LaVergne TN
LVHW060513170826
845677LV00026B/1750

* 9 7 9 8 8 6 9 4 5 1 8 0 4 *